COPYRIGHT

Author Ngogi Emmanuel Mahaye

Ngogi Mahaye's Perspective Quotes

ISBN-978 5536427118

 E-book- ISBN-5536427113

 Copyright Agent

P.O. BOX 81226

Seattle, WA 98108

 USA

Dr

Ngogi

Mahaye

Perspective Quotes

The mind abuse Quotes

Dedication

To my wife, Duduzile 'Queen' Mahaye, my daughters, Dr Nomfundo and
Kusifanelethinasonke, my sons, Amahle, Sicwebisesisonke and Nqobakahlelelizwe, my
brothers, who through their belief in me sacrifice my entire life to the expedition of
educational crusade and ended allowing the will of God to the struggle of our people both
religiously and politically. May I thank their gently inspiration and anticipation emancipated
by immaculate hearts with devine purity ever.

May God revolutionary bless you.

Foreword

I feel very much humbled yet exalted by the noble call embraced by revolution and evolution of ideas that had shaped this exothermic piece of writing dubbed ' Ngogi Mahaye perspective Quotes.

This is a culmination of experiences one encountered in life and its spectrum of life experiments and controls. It stretches your mind to its limit in an endless manner and fashion of its kind. Knowledge is information and information is knowledge but its both transformation tender another version of its matter and energy.

Both knowledge and information as matter and energy cannot be created nor destroyed but merely change from one form to another, hence these unique piece of booklets will change the sober reader from one form to another in the level and position of thinking.

It has been my philosophy and belief to teach an African child like never before and as if you are gun or barrel pointed. This is because they are the future of our liberated country, the hope and future leaders, and the fresh minds of a mindful foresight leadership. The important question is whether they are willing to work hard in order to succeed in getting quality education and go in extra mile putting their concerted effort to acquire skills and talents in ensuring our economic development and growth.

The school going children must be trained to acquire understanding that society of thinkers and its progressive ideas are crucial for them to evolve, and grow to become moral acceptable scholars of a global world. The collection of these quotes in spite of its heterogeneous nature directs to one centre point of focus to spark divergent controversial thinking patterns of its own nature and interpretation. A unified articulation of postcolonial attack to foreign tendencies in all aspect of life tender the processing of any knowledge and information reaches the nation of hope and inherent native pride.

Relevance and time in which it has been published gives impetus to the progressive step of our beloved country South African to advance radical economic transformation and its tenets of securing stable constants increasing economic. This seen in a number of quotes such as "who are you to colonise my mind by prescribing what to think" how to think and what to fall in love with in persuit quality mandatory of our people.

It will promote critical thinking and analytical mode and patriotic tempo in responding to an anxieties raised by growing dark forces to somersault South Africa and Africa for their sustainability of their economic gains in the expense of the poor and the least. This onslaught uses latent old oppressive calculated strategies to woo masses to second pre-1994 pro-imperialist laws and slavery employment opportunities that was assigned to blacks exploitation with small population and its natality than today.

The tremendous change created more social and economic challenges driven by political wave of hope increasing silver lining surface area in the dark cloud the apartheid and colonial regime existed on. It gives me pleasure to reconnect myself and the youth to the real paradigm shift in the political pendulum and academic reflection if not African scholarship resisting inferior position slumbering in terms of economic emancipation and structure. These quotes exist to acquaint the reader about manipulative gratification of evil forces in favour of neo-colonial and neo-liberals suffocating our gains brought by freedom and democracy. Education is exponentially indexed as an apex priority to liberate our mind, hence it is being affectionately defined as a critical phenomenon.

I am putting the work of this nature in the sight of yours aftermath the published books, The Down Trodden Young Brilliant Voices and Education Philosophy Through the Eyes of the Young Ones. It was an enormous task to me as the brainchild and Author of these books as reverence of high esteem.

Ngogi Emmanuel 'Mgogi' Mahaye

"These decades of democracy has brought a variety of mushroom freedom fighters to steal the minds of Mandela children by calling them born frees".

–"Ngogi Mahaye"

"Education is very critical phenomenon that in its nucleus understanding functions as cohesive and adhesive forces to keep world in guttation".
- "Ngogi Mahaye"

"The audience of those who work hard to criticise you destructively will one day form guard of honour and stimulative standing ovation overwhelming saluting your allocates of success in its accord".

–"Ngogi Mahaye"

"We are the beacon of hope for the destitute, the calabash of struggle, the nation and fountain of wisdom
to sprinkle the Germinating
generation through the cross pollination of African philosophy".

- "Ngogi Mahaye"

"My humble background in its sense was terrible, volatile, torturing, careless, and congested with ethnography no one would be proud telling resilience and learnt from downtrodden life, put down walls of architects to surrender our organic line of thinking to the high echelons of oppressors of our forebears".

–"Ngogi Mahaye"

"While I was young my father taught me to be vigilant, firm, humble, industrious and move with constant velocity to avoid malicious compliance in whatever I do for my nation".

- "Ngogi Mahaye"

"Really in reality, ideally in idealistic, I have nothing pragmatic that can sequentially separate me from Him the Most High".

—"Ngogi Mahaye"

"When the strong wind blows, be careful, hold with MUCH FORCE to your tools in whatever I of analysis".

- "Ngogi Mahaye"

"Change is painful but accomodative to soften mind nourished in its grey matter and piameter which is the tender mother of transformation and its tennets of excellence counter paradigm paralysis in progressive shift".

—"Ngogi Mahaye"

"If you make it habitual that you sit in a shoulder of a dwarf, you will enjoy dwarfism and become a good defensive dwarf".

- "Ngogi Mahaye"

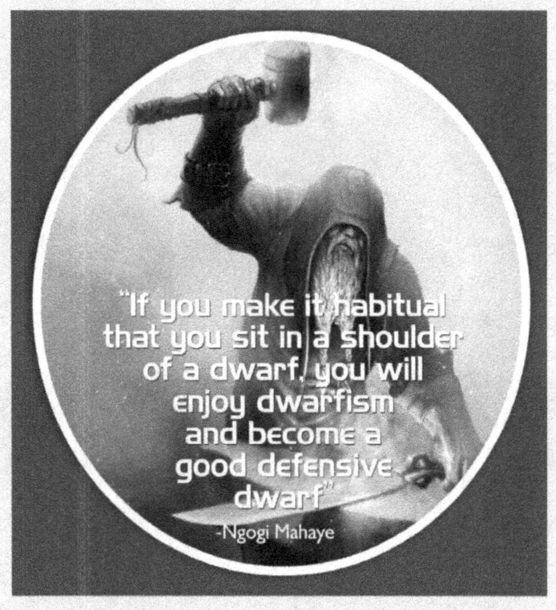

"Counting the distance is a huge mistake of failure furry of the literal idiotism that counts nothing from the spot at the bottom of the heart".

—"Ngogi Mahaye"

"The greatest ambush Of love is its intimacy and aromatic romantism creamed with hypocrisy and latent flirtism".

- "Ngogi Mahaye"

"Too quick to be a liability and too hard to be the asset clearly indicate how difficult this world will be pulled out of imperial economic rulers full of capitalistic mode".

−"Ngogi Mahaye"

"I love what I loved before what is love as the lovable perception to shift any dogmatic paradigm, doctrine about love and its idealistic reality".

- "Ngogi Mahaye"

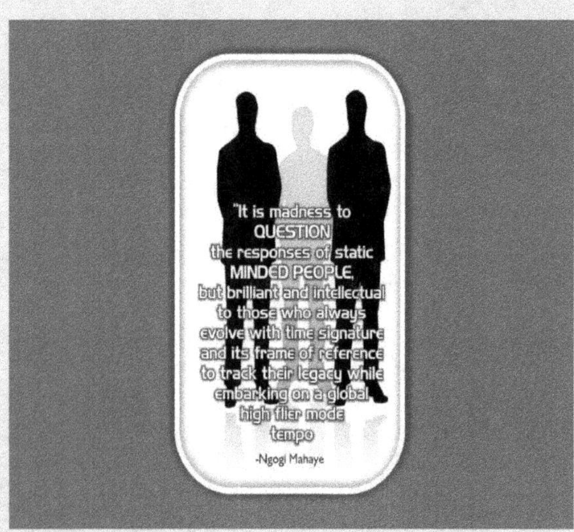

"It is madness to question the response of static MINDED PEOPLE, but brilliant and intellectual to those who always evolve with time signature and its frame of reference to track their legacy while embarking on a global high flier mode tempo".

—"Ngogi Mahaye"

"It is better to deal decisively with the downtrodden attitude of those who still shelter comfortable in the belief that they can banish our economy anger forever when they laurel the graves of our dead".
- "Ngogi Mahaye"

"How on earth the lamb sucks the goat while its own kid suffer on hunger and starvation, it is ridiculous that 'She' the mother of the 'Land' is feeding the lamb which can't be even used in yelling ancestors".

—"Ngogi Mahaye"

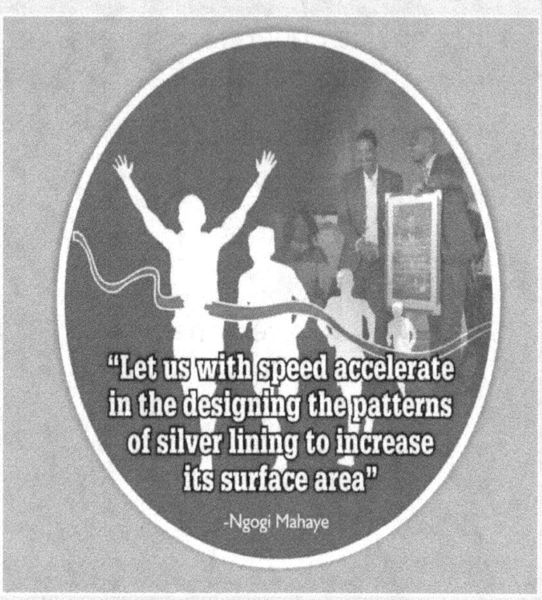

"Let us with speed accelerate in the designing the patterns of silver lining to increase its surface area" - Ngogi 'Mgogi' Mahaye

"Ascending to high position in the echelon of the institutional

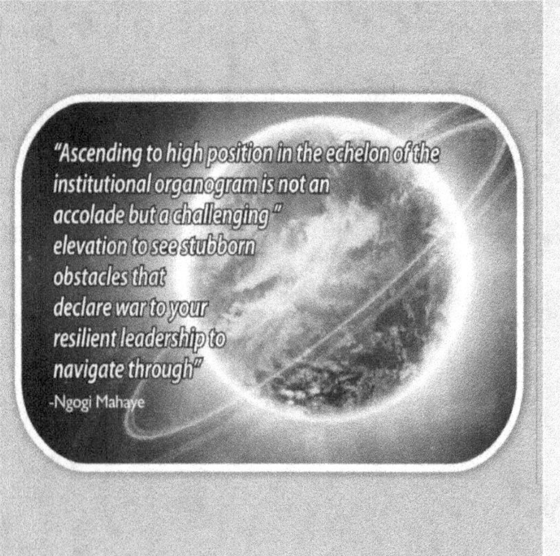

organogram is not an accolade but a challenging elevation to see stubborn obstacles that declare war to your resilient leadership to navigate through".

—"Ngogi Mahaye"

"Any education system that is not putting its learning process at the apex of Socratic questioning and indigenous reflective mirror is a utopian strategy to dwarf their ideas, sideline

learners from intellectual mainstream, caging their cognitive domains in favour of slavery life succumbing to universality of philosophy of African philosophy and its essence to challenge arrogance and sold self-actualization and determination". – "Ngogi Mahaye"

"Vectored people are people for life, life is life. Fight for it".
–"Ngogi Mahaye"

"The darkest hours of colonial and apartheid regime in South Africa brought to table different viewpoints contesting downtrodden mode of thinking of oppressors, their thinking pattern is monological classifying

minds of the blacks as sub-human and replica to animal junk ideas, that stimulated a current reflecting left forces making solid relationship with motive forces of the global community ". – "Ngogi Mahaye"

"The productive learning is the yield of productivity through allowing conflicting ideas and thoughts to center and settle in the transformative tranquility of any society".

—"Ngogi Mahaye"

"When duty calls, we can't be in defiance nor in the myth of laziness. We better die on the line of duty".
—"Ngogi Mahaye"

"Who are you to colonize my mind by prescribing what to think, how to think and what to fall in love with in pursuit of quality mandatory of our people".

—"Ngogi Mahaye"

19

"The xylem and phloem of this earth nowadays needs strong intellectuals to give organic solutions for human tree not to suffer the superfluous claims". –"Ngogi Mahaye"

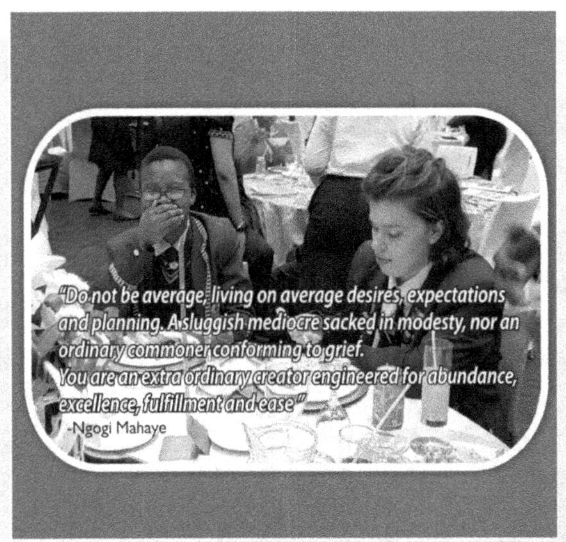

"Do not be average, living on average desires, expectations and planning. A sluggish mediocre sacked in modesty, nor an ordinary commoner conforming to grief. You are an extra ordinary creator engineered for abundance, excellence, fulfillment and ease".   - "Ngogi Mahaye"

"Above the dust beyond the blood, sweat and tears; which are but landmarks on your journey to VICTORY".

-"Ngogi Mahaye"

"Life is like a template that every human being struggle to fit in and sometimes become a replica of a dangerous human form. Let us strive resiliently to modify it to dance to the music that is melodiously and conforming to the calculated risk ever".

- "Ngogi Mahaye"

"Education is very critical phenomenon that in its nucleus understanding functions as cohesive and adhesive forces to keep the world in guttation".

-"Ngogi Mahaye"

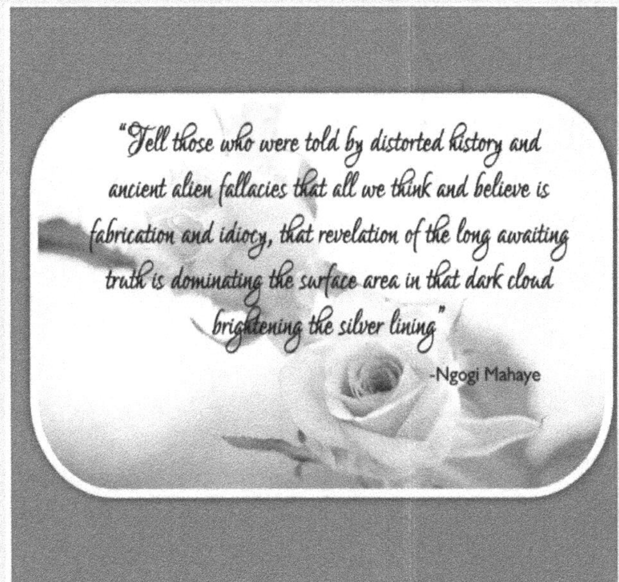

"Tell those who were told by distorted history and ancient alien fallacies that all we think and believe is fabrication and idiocy, that revelation of the long awaiting truth is dominating the surface area in that dark cloud brightening the silver lining".
- "Ngogi Mahaye"

"Our country our future, our organic non contaminated set of ideas to set us all free from the bondage legacy of Non-Socratic colonial regime".

-"Ngogi Mahaye"

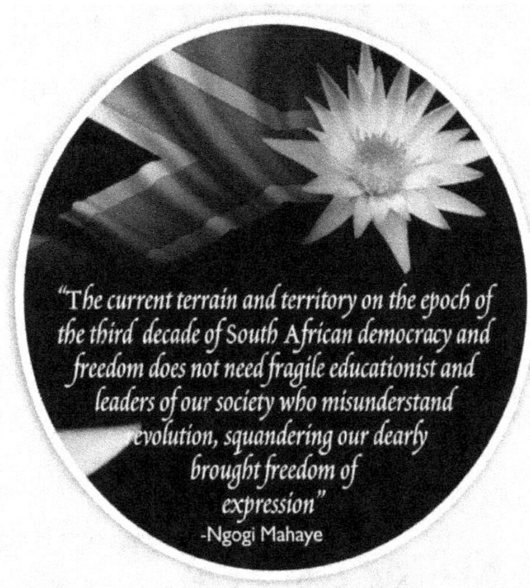

"The current terrain and territory on the epoch of the third decade of South African democracy and freedom does not need fragile educationist and leaders who misunderstand evolution, squandering our dearly brough freedom of expression"

- "Ngogi Mahaye"

"If your thoughts are insoluble, test its concentration or its state versus nature as no analysis of one's mind be an outcast of it's genuine radical source".

- "Ngogi Mahaye"

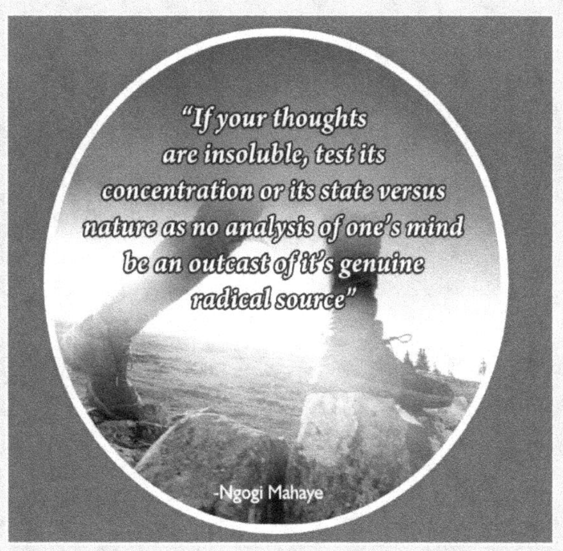

"Put comma not full stop and move forward with speed at the end no one guaranteed lifetime stay in this earth; we are all going to perform that last chromatic beat to greet the unknown world".

-"Ngogi Mahaye"

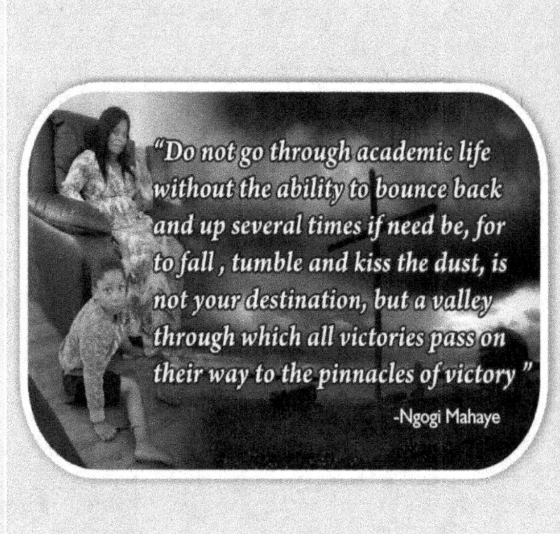

"Do not go through academic life without the ability to bounce back and up several times if need be, for to fall, tumble and kiss the dust, is not your destination, but a valley through which all victories pass on their way to the pinnacles of victory".

-"Ngogi Mahaye"

"When the black cloud carrying intellectual starvation, political poverty, leadership decay, misleading and squandering what our forebears fought for by taking detour on white monopoly capital to sustain socio economic status quo benefitting the minority of the African population".

- "Ngogi Mahaye"

"Tell me what is never told, I will salute you, a   nd tell me in your dialectical   if not dialogical   what was told I will forever   respect you".

-"Ngogi Mahaye"

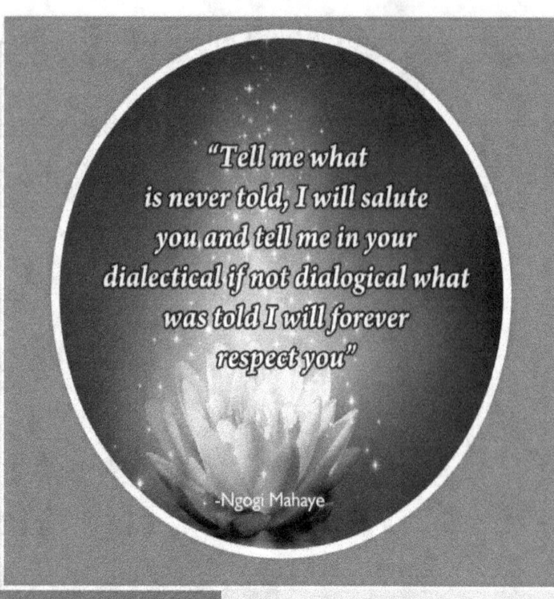

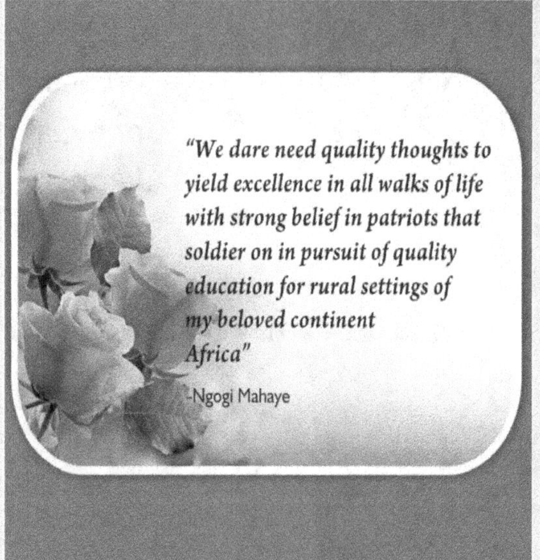

"We dare need quality thoughts to yield excellence in all walks of life with strong belief in patriots that soldier on in pursuit of quality education for rural settings of my beloved continent Africa".

-"Ngogi Mahaye"

"If
you enjoy
work, you
are not at
work, if
you still
finds
discomfort
at work,
you are
still not at
work, but
if you are serious,
and use all
calculated means to
be serious, you will
find peace of
mind".

"Ngogi Mahaye"

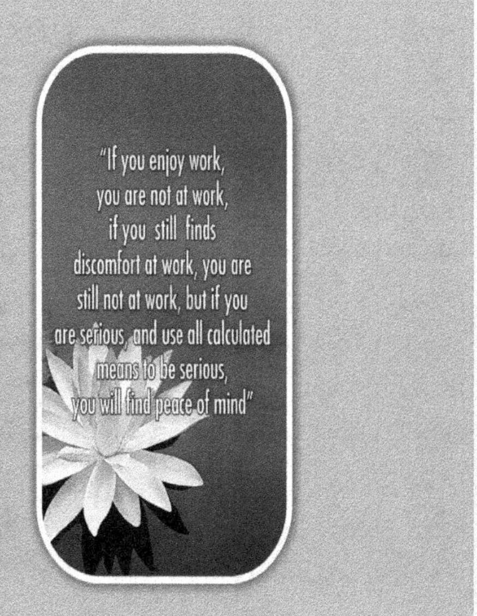

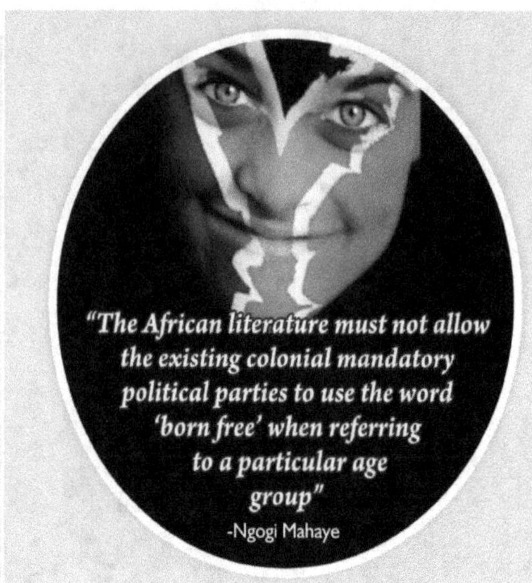

"The African literature must not allow the existing colonial mandatory political parties to use the word 'born free' when referring to a particular age group".

-"Ngogi Mahaye"

"The lyrics of African renaissance perforate the black porosity and filtrate youth glomerules to mentally excrete inferiority complex that tarnished their native inherent".

-"Ngogi Mahaye"

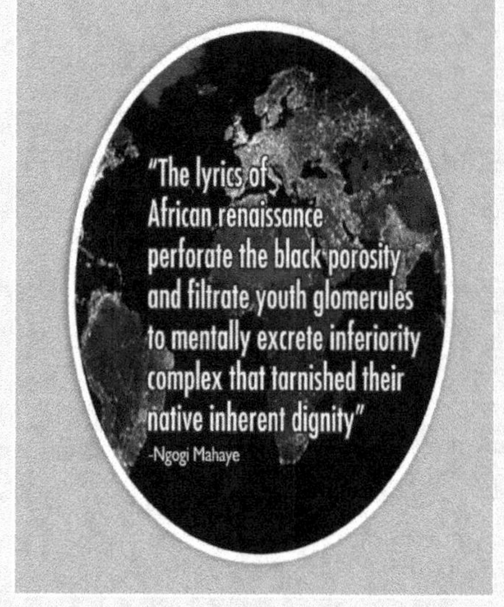

"The only world recognized continent carrying compound nucleus of critical philosophy of caring through coexistence in the ecosystems of ideas, thoughts and non-faked relationship is Africa through 'Ubuntu' ".

- "Ngogi Mahaye"

"There is no lotto of ideas and thoughts but quench for wells of its think tankers".
-"Ngogi Mahaye"

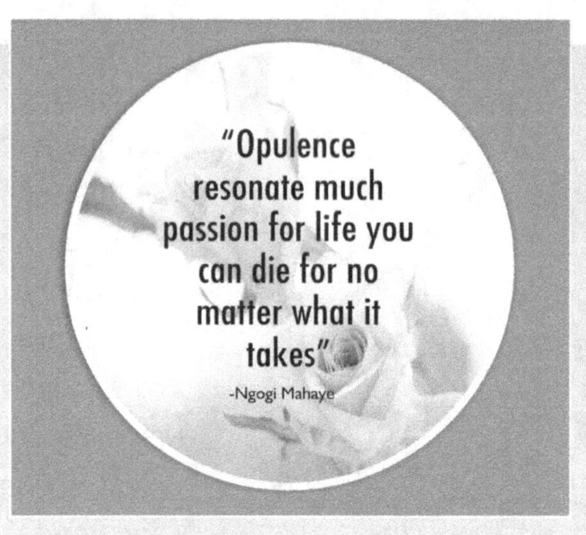

"Opulence
resonate much
passion for life you
can die for no
matter what it
takes".

-"Ngogi Mahaye"

"Ambition and
conviction can be
created nor
destroyed but like
matter and energy
merely changes
from one state to
another".

-"Ngogi Mahaye"

"The opaque
glass is literal
better than
chaotic
speeches".
-"Ngogi Mahaye"

"Chaotic
gestures
speaks
louder than
chaotic
speeches".
 - "Ngogi
    Mahaye"

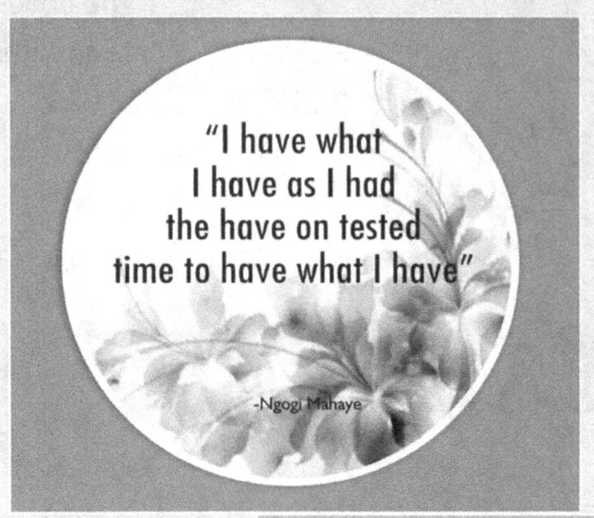

"I have what I have as I had the have on tested time to what I have".

-"Ngogi Mahaye"

"The youth must learn to understand the understood and bring innovations, creativity and invent inventions moving forward".

- "Ngogi Mahaye"

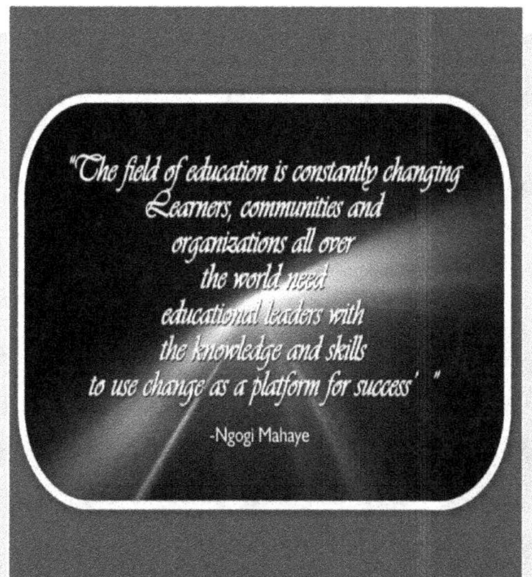

"The field of education is constantly changing learners, communities and organizations all over the world need educational leaders with the knowledge and skills to use change as a platform for success".

"Laurels symbolizes great accomplishments of high accolades but a huge curse when you begin to end it by resting constantly on them with your defensive mode of thinking".

-"Ngogi Mahaye"

"If it is not me is I and if it is not I is mine, so I am whom you beg to differ since uniqueness characterize my reputation".

-"Ngogi Mahaye"

"Good leaders come from anywhere but great leaders rise from the humble backgrounds and pass through tribulation and starvation to conquer the world".

- "Ngogi Mahaye"

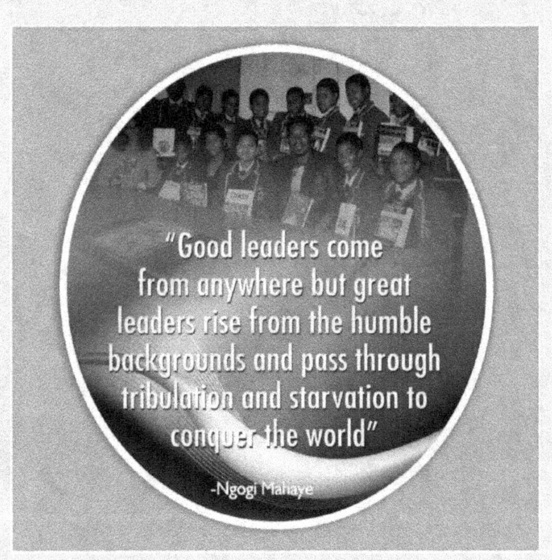

36

"If you are not RESPONSIBLE for something you are responsible for anything to any direction even to hell".

-"Ngogi Mahaye"